THIS BOOK
BELONGS TO:

Birth date:

Birth time:

Birth location:

ZODIAC SIGNS

PISCES

ZODIAC SIGNS

PISCES

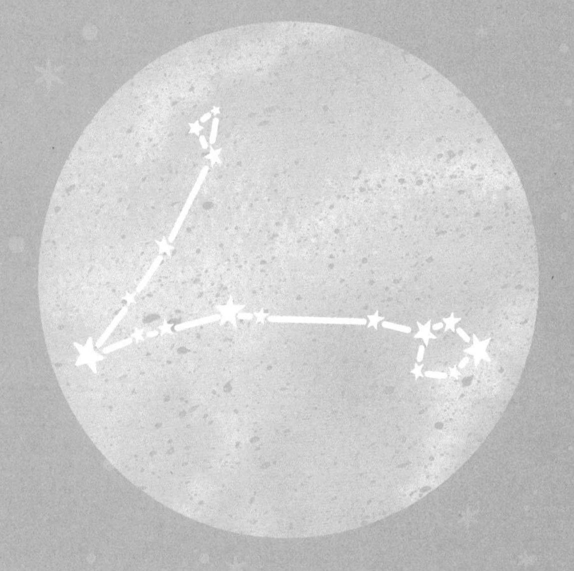

SHAKIRAH TABOURN

STERLING ETHOS
New York

An Imprint of Sterling Publishing Co., Inc.
1166 Avenue of the Americas
New York, NY 10036

ISBN 978-1-4549-3896-5

Distributed in Canada by Sterling Publishing Co., Inc.
c/o Canadian Manda Group, 664 Annette Street
Toronto, Ontario M6S 2C8, Canada
Distributed in the United Kingdom by GMC Distribution Services
Castle Place, 166 High Street, Lewes, East Sussex BN7 1XU, England
Distributed in Australia by NewSouth Books
University of New South Wales, Sydney, NSW 2052, Australia

For information about custom editions, special sales, and premium and corporate purchases, please contact Sterling Special Sales at 800-805-5489 or specialsales@sterlingpublishing.com.

Manufactured in China

2 4 6 8 10 9 7 5 3 1

sterlingpublishing.com

Cover design by Elizabeth Mihaltse Lindy
Cover and endpaper illustration by Sarah Frances
Interior design by Nancy Singer
Zodiac signs © wikki33 and macrovector/freepik

Dedicated to my Nana, Mary Brown, the first Pisces
to enter my world. In addition, this is for all of the
amazing Pisces in my life. Thank you all for showing me
the value of compassion, intuition, and magic on Earth.

CONTENTS

INTRODUCTION

To understand Pisces, the twelfth sign of the zodiac, you must first understand the eleven signs that precede it. The zodiac itself is a literal expanse of constellations that form a belt around our cosmos. It can be imagined as the backdrop of the story that the celestial bodies play out before us. The zodiac is also a spectrum, symbolic of our life cycle, with energy that pervades everything we know.

Aries, the sign that begins the zodiac (in most traditions), represents the beginning of life—birth, the moment we actualize as human beings separate from the womb. This fiery sign is therefore associated with the separation of the self from others. Its phrase is "I am," and its energy is forward moving, in a straight direction, like a newborn emerging from the womb. Through the next ten signs of the zodiac, we see the development of values in Taurus, communication in Gemini, comfort and security in Cancer, creativity in

Leo, service in Virgo, partnership in Libra, loss in Scorpio, belief in Sagittarius, purpose in Capricorn, and community in Aquarius. In Pisces, we encounter an energy that can be described as compassionate and empathetic, sincere and heartfelt. Its presence as the final sign of the zodiac belt—the one that comes after life, but before (re)birth—is somewhat mysterious and often misunderstood. There are good reasons for this! As the final sign, Pisces holds some of life's deepest mysteries—the realm of illusion and delusion, faeries, mystical beings, spirits, and angels. Pisces is a world of universal love that exists between Earth and spirit at all times, and those born under this sign have the ability to tap into its energy whenever they need to.

Pisces is a sign frequently associated with Jesus Christ through the symbols of the fish and the feet. The symbol of Pisces is two fish swimming in opposite directions, representing the different currents that Pisces are pulled toward at any given time, as well as the inherent duality in the sign. Jesus is also often associated with fish for many reasons, one being that he is said to have fed 5,000 people with two fish and five loaves of bread. Feet are the body part ruled by Pisces. In the Bible, Jesus washes the feet of his disciples, showing his dedication to a life of service. Pisces are often said to have Christlike spirits, and the souls of the people born under this sign seem to gravitate toward service and compassion. Pisces tend to operate from a fundamental sense of empathy. It's not uncommon for Pisces to believe that they've already lived many lives. Perhaps this is why Pisces can empathize so well with other people and why they often give the impression that they've walked many miles in other people's shoes. Indeed, this empathy is a strong argument in favor of reincarnation. The basic idea here is that, because Pisces have experienced so many different lives through reincarnation, their souls possess an expanded view of what life on Earth is all about. Their deep understanding and acceptance of others often leads people to describe them as "old souls," even when they are young.

Pisces possess deep emotional knowledge and strong intuition, as their sensitive bodies and souls can pick up on subtleties in the air and people around them that others simply don't recognize. Pisces can look at people on the street and sense their stresses, problems, and sufferings, though they can't explain this phenomenon. They may not know specific details about others, but they have general intuitive hunches. Through simple interactions, Pisces who have honed their intuitive skills can often pinpoint specific locations in the body experiencing pain or uncover the emotional troubles someone is dealing with. This doesn't necessarily mean they're all psychic (although many are), but they all have the ability to use their intuitive energy in this way. Intuition is the bedrock of Pisces' ability to move through the world. They must learn that their intuition is like a muscle; continuous practice is the only way to strengthen it. This can lead to a lot of pain and confusion during the teenage and young adult years. As their brains develop during this critical time, it can be difficult to discern truth from deception, love from infatuation, or intuition from intrusive thoughts. The earlier they are taught to honor their intuitive hunches and trust themselves, the better off they'll be. Of course, this isn't foolproof! There will be plenty of mistakes made, tears shed, and hearts broken throughout Pisces' lifetime. Despite all this, they cannot abandon their intuition—it's their greatest strength and their secret weapon. They are here to experience all of life—the highs and the lows—and they ride through these changes like the waves of the ocean.

And just like the ocean, Pisces are known for their immense depth and expansive nature. Their strength is in their watery essence—their ability to transcend earthly boundaries through deep emotional knowledge and a spiritual mindset. Their moods wax and wane continuously each day, changing like the ocean's tides. The truth is that they can experience an influx of emotions at any given time, from any number of random stimuli. This is a result of their immense sensitivity. They're often referred to as sponges, as they tend to soak up the memories, words, and energies of the people and places they associate with on a daily basis. A Pisces might hear a song playing in the grocery store and become overwhelmed with emotion. This can happen if the song brings them back to a tender memory from childhood. Or perhaps they go out with a friend who can't stop complaining about their significant other. Pisces might return home feeling extremely tired, as if they've spent all their energy. Even if they've had a relaxing day otherwise, the mere act of sharing space with a person in turmoil can bring their energy down. Pisces learn the effects of taking on other people's energies throughout their lives, and it's a constant struggle for them to maintain personal boundaries. Pisces are inherently boundless. They need to be free to ride the waves of the ocean of life.

MUTABLE SIGNS

Also like the ocean, Pisces is a mutable sign, meaning its energy is changeable, adaptable, flowing, and fluctuating. Mutability is a characteristic of Pisces' modality—the quality of energy by which a sign operates. There are three other mutable signs: Gemini, Virgo, and Sagittarius. A helpful way to categorize the modality of a sign is to take note of the quality of the weather during the thirty days that the sun is in one of the signs mentioned above. They share a number of inconsistencies. During Gemini season, spring changes to summer (in the Northern Hemisphere). There are cold days, hot days, and in-between days. The weather can't be properly categorized as either spring or summer quite yet. In Virgo season, a similar transition happens, this time from summer to fall. The weather begins to cool down, but exceptionally warm days are still interspersed throughout the season. In Sagittarius season, the shift is from autumn to winter. The final leaves begin to fall off the trees, animals begin to slow down and move into hibernation, and humans begin to switch from light jackets to winter coats. When the sun is in Pisces, the season begins to change from winter to spring. A thawing occurs. The weather moves back and forth between sunshine and windy, wintry days.

Pisces, like the other mutable signs, ushers in the changing of the seasons. These signs always precede an equinox or solstice. They therefore help prepare us for the major turning points of the year. Pisces gets us ready for the spring equinox—the moment when the sun moves across the equator, marked by a day in which the daytime is equal to the night. The spring equinox can be seen as a rebirth of sorts, as it takes place when the sun leaves Pisces and enters Aries, the beginning of the zodiac. Pisces therefore possesses energy that spurs growth. It is the space between thresholds, suspended between endings and beginnings. It can be thought of as the chrysalis of a butterfly, meaning the time just before the butterfly emerges from its cocoon. Pisces holds space for transformations to occur, providing a safe container to completely dissolve into nothingness and reemerge as something brand new.

NEPTUNE ENERGY

It is worth mentioning that Neptune, a far-out planet often associated with Pisces, has been moving through the sign since April of 2011. It will remain there until late January of 2026. Neptune's influence in Pisces cannot be overlooked. It heightens and intensifies the significations of the sign as it slowly makes its way to the end of the zodiac. Piscean children born under this influence will have heightened sensitivities and intuitive powers, as well as a greater propensity toward Neptunian delusions. Neptune acts to spiritualize the sign it is moving through, dissolving boundaries and creating illusions, fantasies, and out-of-this-world experiences. It shows us that separation is the biggest illusion there is, that everything that ever was is one, and that we are all connected, always. Neptunian energy means universal love consciousness. The wavelength that it vibrates on connects the hearts of all living beings.

But it doesn't always emit love and good vibes! Neptunian energy can be quite destructive, and not all structures should be destroyed. Neptune has the potential to leave us completely blinded toward the truths dangling right in front of our faces. There are deeper lessons to this planet, but they usually aren't revealed until long after its effects have worn off. Neptune in Pisces has affected our culture at large in many ways, some good, some harmful. One aspect of Neptune in Pisces is the continued growth in popularity of spiritual practices and traditions. People around the world are beginning to search for deeper connections to a force larger than themselves outside of traditional religions. A downside of Neptune's influence has been the rise in addiction to pharmaceuticals and opioids. With Neptune in Pisces, the propensity to "check out" from life is strong, as both Neptune and Pisces significations allude to the need to remove oneself from the harshness of reality. A whole generation of children has been born to addicted parents, and we've yet to see the long-term effects this will have on their psyches.

BEFORE YOU BEGIN

As you dive into this book, keep in mind that there is so much more to astrology than your Sun sign! If you've ever had the magical experience of seeing your birth chart—or even better, of receiving a reading from a professional astrologer—you probably already have an idea of how vast the subject matter is. A birth chart is a two-dimensional map of the heavens at the time of your birth. In other words, it acts as a roadmap, guide, or blueprint for your life. It shows the entire zodiac belt and the location of each of the planets at the given time of birth, and each planet holds its own special meaning! Additionally, it describes the conversations taking place among the planets through the geometric angles they make in relation to each other. These angles are called aspects. The birth chart shows the sign and planets that were rising in the East and setting in the West at the time of birth, and which signs and planets were high above you in the sky or below the Earth when you came into this world. Yes, all of this has meaning! You'll be able to learn about your rising sign, your Moon sign, your Mercury and Venus signs, and so much more!

The good news is, you can see your entire chart for free online, and it's even possible to research a few simple delineations. A great place to start is astro.com; however, it is best to consult a professional astrologer if possible to help give context to the information you find on the internet. Visit your local metaphysical store for a selection of books and reading materials to get you started if you're really interested in learning more! Astrology is an invaluable tool that can help you in myriad ways, some of which include learning self-acceptance, getting in tune with the timing of your life, and being able to better understand others.

This book will resonate with you if your Sun sign, Moon sign, or Rising sign is Pisces. After reading this, you may also want to purchase the books that correlate with your other signs. That way you'll develop a fuller picture of your specific attunements!

Many of you reading this book are Pisces Suns, but some may be Pisces Moons or Risings! Here's an explanation of all three and the differences between them:

SUN SIGN

The Sun illuminates wherever it shines its rays. You are the Sun in your life, casting rays synonymous with the particular unique shade of your Sun sign. The sun represents your essential self, your central personality, your vitality, who you came here to be, how you shine, your self-expression, and the energy you need to recharge with.

If you were born while the sun was in Pisces, your primary mode of being is compassionate and creative. You are someone whose self-expression is based on feeling and tuning into your intuition to navigate the world around you. You came here to help people, to guide people toward self-healing, and to use your creativity to share your elaborate fantasies with others. Emotional connections fuel your soul, and creativity and world-building come easy to you. You are gifted with the ability to see through the lines and tap into other realms of existence through just being you! Rest and regeneration are wildly important for Pisces Suns, as your energy is often scattered in many directions. Rest will refuel you so that you can shine brightly once again.

MOON SIGN

The Moon is our constant reminder of the past; a piece of the Earth that long, long ago detached and became flung into orbit around our Earth. The Moon, therefore, represents where you come from, your roots, home, and family, as well as your internal and emotional self. It's your intuition and instincts, what you need to feel nurtured and cared for, and how you do the same for yourself and others. The Moon also represents what feels comfortable, safe, and natural for you.

If you were born while the Moon was in Pisces, you are a sweet and sensitive soul. Your emotional currents run deep, and you may have a hard time differentiating between your emotions and others'. Your instinctual reactions tend to be deeply felt within your psyche, which means it can often take a while to fully process what's happening. In order to feel safe and comfortable, you need to be able to feel like you can escape the intensity of the world around you. You may decorate your home or room so that it feels like a space to retreat to within your environment. Escapes of some sort are necessary for Pisces of all types, but especially Pisces Moons! Making art, watching movies, reading stories, exploring nature, and meditation are some examples of healthy ways to retreat from the world around you.

RISING SIGN

Also known as the Ascendant, the Rising Sign is the sign that was rising on the eastern horizon at the time of birth. To figure out your rising sign, you have to know the time, place, and location of birth. The eastern horizon represents the point where the sky meets the earth, or where spirit meets matter, and represents the energy that a person's life begins with. Your Rising Sign is the general vibe that you give out to the world. It's the energy you move about the world with, and it's how others perceive you, as it's the first layer of the personality that people encounter in others. The Rising Sign will point to what you look like, how you dress, and how you show up in the world. It represents you at your highest and best self. It's your temperament and outward personality.

If you have a Pisces Rising, you'll find that people of all types are drawn to you like magnets! This is because Pisces Rising people appear to be so open and empathetic to others. Because Pisces is a water sign, you might give off an energy that shows others that you are caring and compassionate, which is super alluring to most people! As a Pisces Rising, you may also give off an elusive and mystical vibe, seeming to embody out-of-this-world energy to those that meet them. This can be seen in the way you dress and interact with people. You may be described as "Zen," "chill," or "so sweet!" by others. There is an air of mystery, glamor, and fantasy about you that others find intriguing. You may find that you're extremely sensitive to the people around you and the environments you inhabit, as your outer layer (rising sign) is so elusive and boundless. Be sure to find ample time to retreat, re-center, and ground your energy when you're feeling tired and worn out.

This book is suitable for Pisces Suns, Moons, and Risings, as it will give you a helpful perspective about the energy you inhabit every day, and useful tips on how to work with it instead of against it.

PISCES

as a Child

Pisces children contain the purest forms of energy—imagination, creativity, and especially sensitivity. Pisces children born between April 2011 and January 2026 also have the addition of Neptune in their sign, which means they have an especially sensitive disposition. Neptune's influence is similar to Pisces' nature in that it sensitizes, spiritualizes, and dissolves boundaries. These children will find Piscean themes to be especially potent in their personalities.

All Pisces possess a necessary need for escape. This need stems directly from their immense sensitivity! The world is perceived as entirely too harsh for the sensitive Piscean soul. Therefore, retreat of some sort is necessary in order to cope with the reality of incarnation. In Piscean children, this often looks like long periods of play in fantasy worlds, watching movies, or getting lost in artistic activities such as drawing or painting. You'll find a Pisces child engaging in these activities as a form of play, but they also serve as ways to cope with the complexities they might face at home, such as arguing or upset parents. These children are so sensitive that they can pick up on the energies of others regardless of how hard they may try to hide them. Actually, it's best not to try and hide feelings and emotions from Pisces. This only results in mixed signals, which can lead to confusion. The Pisces child will think, *I know Daddy is upset about this, but he keeps telling me everything is okay.* These children can easily internalize passive-aggressive behavior and interpret it as being their fault. Instead, a simple explanation is much easier for them to process. *Mommy is upset because of x,y,z, but I want you to know that none of that is your fault or for you to worry about. You're so sweet for being concerned about me, and I appreciate it.* These children react very poorly to angry and aggressive communication and tend to shut down and retreat further into their preferred methods of escape when confronted in this way.

In addition to the need for regular escape, the need for a protected physical space to express themselves in is just as important. This cannot be stressed enough! The Piscean child needs space within their home to feel safe, held, and contained. Without this, they will most likely be unable to fully and freely express themselves. This sacred space should be their own, free from the rest of the family's clutter. Even if it is only a small closet or a corner of a room, it should be their private area, safe and secure enough for them to slip into their own world. They will probably find this place by themselves, through their own explorations around the home. Wherever they end up, be sure that they feel no shame about their choice. This is their area of safety, where they'll continuously retreat to throughout their childhood (and possibly beyond). Everyone deserves such a space, no matter their age.

Additionally, Pisces needs a steady connection to nature. If this isn't available at home, then make sure they have ample time and opportunities to play in parks, explore the woods, or lie next to bodies of water. Pisces are connected to the subtler energies around us, and nature helps ground what may be excesses in our energy fields. This is essential for any Pisces, but especially for children, who are so open and impressionable. Ample time in nature is also an important part of Pisces' learning process. They learn best through direct experience, through their senses, and with their hands. They will most likely enjoy learning about nature—trees, the four elements, gardening, animals, etc. They usually prefer to have direct, hands-on experiences with that they're learning. If you're teaching them about the cycle of seed to plant, you better have a seed ready for them to plant and watch grow! Piscean children take their time when learning a subject. They'll do it at their own pace and can't be rushed toward a quick understanding. Again, this is why direct experience with the given subject is helpful, as it allows them to absorb the information easier. The Pisces child wants to learn all the time, as they enjoy the process of collecting information from everything around them. This is comforting and safe for Pisces, who loves to be curious, ask questions, and learn. Because their subtle bodies are always picking up information from what's around them, speaking their curiosities out loud helps them build new neural pathways. So, there should be plenty of books and educational tools at home. They learn more at home than at school most of the time, as their home space is where they integrate what they've learned in the classroom. They read through books in a breeze, so frequent trips to the local public library are also very helpful! They feel a special kind of safety and comfort surrounded by books. They love becoming lost in the fantasy that books provide, and they can easily become emotionally attached to the characters they read about, even going as far as to embody their personalities while steeped in their world. In addition to books, TV shows and movies are other comfortable sources of escape for Pisces of all ages.

The Pisces child will have a special relationship with the family pet, whether it's a fish, a cat, a dog, or a lizard. Pets are connected to Virgo in astrology, the sign opposite of Pisces. Therefore, Piscean children feel a particular affinity for and magnetism toward animals. They're sympathetic to animals of all kinds, communicating with them almost telepathically. Tarot enthusiasts might look toward the Page of Cups, often depicted as a young person communicating with a fish. It's almost as though little Pisces can tap into another realm that contains the thoughts and feelings of their animal friends. A pet allows a young Pisces to learn responsibility early on, as they are already empathetic to the basic needs of animals. The daily routine of feeding, walking, or caring for a pet is helpful and healing to Pisces' soul, as being grounded in routine helps balance out the propensity for too much escape. Their pet will be their very best friend, and it will bring out their capacity for love and compassion early on in life. Pisces has the unique ability to love everyone and everything on a soul level, and this trait will manifest in how the Pisces child acts toward their pet.

It isn't uncommon for Pisces children to have food sensitivities, which are often caused by their sensitive bodies. Whether this means a serious allergy, stomachaches, hives, or just a strong distaste for particular foods, it's important to honor the given sensitivity. The worst thing for a Pisces child to hear is that they're crazy or that their intuitions about their own body are wrong. This can lead to an eventual distrust of the self and their decision-making capabilities. Instead, work with them in concert with their doctor(s) to learn more about their sensitivities. It is highly important that a young Pisces is given a healthy diet with low amounts of added sugars and caffeine, as these can prove to be overly stimulating for such sensitive kiddos. It's also important that they aren't criticized for their eating habits or food intake. A young Pisces will internalize any negative talk about food or their body, and as a result, they could learn to be uncomfortable with their body early on. This can lead to Pisces disassociating from their body at a young age, potentially causing depression or disordered eating practices that can take a lot of effort, therapy, and time to heal.

A Pisces child is similar to a Pisces adult—they just want to love and be loved! That is the core of their needs. Lead with your heart with these children, as they need to be in tune with emotions. Their parents are the mirrors by which they learn emotional intelligence. There is no such thing as a perfect parent, but the Pisces child will see and recognize efforts made on their behalf. What these kids need most of all, besides displays of unconditional love, is structure. Their parents need to be able to provide a strong, reliable foundation rooted in compassion rather than punishment. If this is created, the young Pisces will grow to maintain their empathy and loving spirit while also developing balance and maturity.

PISCES

as an Adult

An adult Pisces might find that they move through life aimlessly and without direction until their Saturn Return hits, which is usually between the ages of twenty-eight and thirty. The Saturn Return is when the planet Saturn makes its way back to where it was initially when a person was born. This period, lasting about three years, marks a time of major maturity and growth. We are forced to make decisions and lay the groundwork of our adult lives. Before this time, Pisces can be found holding onto lofty ideals, unsure of where life is taking them. They tend to shuttle from job to job and relationship to relationship, with no real direction or sense of purpose. The Saturn Return forces them to become aware of the reality of their situation and life path and makes them realize that it is time to solidify plans for the future. A major part of learning life's lessons is facing the reality of incarnating into the physical body. This is rough for everyone, but especially for Pisces, who has a difficult time facing reality. Pisces is a rather ethereal sign, one that can easily disengage with reality and live in a fantasy world. It prefers that world to real-life horrors and responsibilities. During the Saturn Return, Pisces is forced to face the realities of being in a physical body on this earthly plane! There is no real way to escape other than death.

Pisces' opposite sign, Virgo, puts this in perspective. Virgo, a mutable Earth sign, is all about physical incarnation, work, health, and learning to live in the body. Virgo rules routines and physicality, lifestyle development, and everything we do to function on a day-to-day basis. Pisces can often deny these parts of life, preferring fantasy and illusion to the mundanity of everyday living. The Saturn Return forces Pisces to accept this reality one way or another. There needs to be room for both the mystical and the mundane! When Pisces is finally able to realize this, they can truly begin to create magic in their everyday life. The Saturn Return humbles and humanizes Pisces in a very real way. Looking at the full birth chart is necessary to paint a more accurate picture of the areas of life the Saturn Return will affect the most, but in general it usually touches every aspect of a person's life. The sobering part of this time is most noteworthy, as Pisces aren't typically known for being sober!

Pisces experience deep pain when they sit with reality for too long. They tend to view it as too limiting and harsh, and they can be rather fatalistic in their views of life on Earth. To cope with this pain, Pisces pursues escape by any means necessary. As a child, escape might look like extended periods of play, becoming lost in the fantasies provided by movies and books, spending a long time outdoors, or engaging with nature. However, the pressures of adulthood make these types of escape seem out of reach, especially for Pisces with demanding day jobs, unsatisfying personal relationships, or feelings of uncertainty and hopelessness. Many turn to other forms of escape, such as drinking, recreational drug use, retail therapy, endless social media scrolling, or mindless Internet surfing. Often these things go hand in hand. Numbing the pain of incarnation is both necessary and destructive. The truth is, there is no hiding from reality no matter how hard one tries. Alcohol, drugs, and other forms of temporary escape are just that—temporary. The high never lasts, and Pisces are left in a cycle of numbing pain, dissociation, guilt, regret, and repetition. It becomes less about facing the reality of incarnation and more about hiding from the self. Addiction of one sort or another is common among Pisces. The same is also true for people with Pisces Moons, as their instinctual reaction when faced with any kind of discomfort is to find escape.

The Saturn Return shatters the illusions of addiction and substance abuse in major ways. This period of time takes place over a few years, so its full story is bound to be a long one. It is likely that Pisces will first begin to notice ways in which their life can no longer continue in the direction it's headed. However, they will likely be in denial about it. A Pisces has incredible intuition, but they very often doubt it! They know what needs to change, but they won't be able to acknowledge it head-on for some time.

As the Saturn Return progresses, what they've realized will become more and more difficult to ignore. Loved ones will begin to notice, too, likely because whatever they're denying has by this time become a more obvious problem pushed to the forefront of the psyche. As time progresses, it is very likely that Pisces will continue to try to ignore or push back on this core issue, preferring to remain in denial until they absolutely can't any longer. The best way to handle this time in their lives is by being brave enough to face the realities of growing up in a physical body. They must attempt to live life within certain structures and boundaries. Once Pisces comes to understand that boundaries can be loving containers of growth and experience, they begin to experience a sense of freedom that they never knew existed!

Suffering is a real part of incarnation, and it is something Pisces in particular must reckon with in this lifetime. To be a Pisces is to know suffering, to witness the abuses and sorrows of the world, to feel the aching Earth within the self, and to somehow choose to continue to see the divine in everything. That optimistic view is the ultimate life purpose for Pisces! The Saturn Return shows them the importance of embracing this reality. They have the ability to truly help others with their suffering, but to do so they must acknowledge its existence and its potential to be changed. Through this process, Pisces has to reckon with the choices they've made so far in life and decide if the road they're on is leading them toward the life they want. If not, how can this be addressed? Should Pisces pivot in another direction entirely or wander off course slightly and explore until they find their way back to the main road? The process of undoing can be heartbreaking and difficult to move through, as it involves a breakdown of previous ways of living. It is one thing to quit drinking, for example, but it's another to let go of the weekly hangouts at the bar with coworkers on Friday nights, or to have to isolate oneself from certain friends and situations to stay sober. A total recalibration must take place once Pisces is ready to commit to changing their lifestyle, and suffering comes into play once again. They may have a breakdown when they realize how *boring* life becomes once their everyday escape has been removed, as this forces them to find meaning in the mundane. The best remedy for this is nature. Returning back to the Earth always stabilizes an otherwise restless Pisces. Meditation is also essential. This is true for life in general, but it's particularly true for troubling and confusing periods like the Saturn Return.

It is way too easy for Pisces to get stuck in their heads, running through feedback loops of despair. Worry constantly plagues the Piscean mind, which leads them to self-medication and escapist behaviors. They want to avoid the reality of a potentially meaningless life. To move through this is notably difficult, as the Saturn Return is often the undoing of the spirit in order to reach new depths of understanding about the meaning of life. Hopefully, after the Saturn Return, Pisces is able to find meaning and a newfound understanding of what it means to live in a human body on this Earth. Yes, suffering is inevitable, but so is beauty, love, magic, and connection. The Saturn Return shows Pisces how necessary their contribution to the world around them is. This period helps Pisces understand that every part of life is necessary to make the whole, including the ugly, dark parts and the beautiful, uplifting ones. They begin to understand that suffering can be recategorized as tolerance.

PISCES

as a Parent

The healthy Pisces parent is a natural caregiver. They want to foster and try to maintain an innocence in their children while striving to adequately prepare them for the "real world" and adulthood. With their sensitivity toward life in general, the Pisces parent is acutely aware of the dangers and grievances of being born in this world. They'll do their best to both protect their child from the hurtful things they have had to experience and prepare them for every challenge imaginable—an impossible feat! What the Piscean parent has to remember is that their child is inheriting some of their patterning, no matter how much they try to shield them from it. In fact, the more they try to protect their child from experiencing the ups and downs of life, the worse off they'll be.

For many Pisces parents, parenting can be a true joy—something they feel they were born to do. In their eyes, the goal is to raise conscious, empathetic, intelligent individuals who will continue to uplift the Earth. The act of birthing and bringing life into this world is a deeply spiritual act for those who choose to do so, and this is why many opt for more natural birthing methods. The Pisces child-bearer may be found researching a lot about natural births, herbal symptom remediation, organic foods, and the best methods to remove harmful chemicals from the home and diet. They can easily become caught up in the fantasy of "the perfect birth," which helps distract them from their underlying fears about childbirth and parenthood. Hiring a doula for all stages of pregnancy can be extremely helpful for Pisces and their stress levels. A doula is a person hired to advocate for the needs of the pregnant person and provide them with support. This means support during the pregnancy, birth, and oftentimes postpartum. Having an extra anchor of support is crucial for Pisces, as they often doubt themselves and have trouble advocating for themselves while under stress. In addition, Pisces feels safer and more comfortable with someone who is able to hold space for them and cater to their needs without their having to ask for it directly. This is because Pisces especially doesn't like to be a bother. A doula is an integral member of the birthing team, giving the Piscean parent a container, a pillar, and someone who will fight for them when necessary. While fears around childbirth are completely normal, oftentimes a Pisces will allow their fears to spin out of control. A doula can help with this as well. They try to continuously bring Pisces back down to Earth with facts that ground their spirits. This is especially important when birthing time comes around. By then, Pisces has normally absorbed as much information as possible about childbirth and parenthood, and this can lead to even more stress.

Given their watery nature and connection to the pre-birth phase of life, Pisces sometimes opt for water births. Another birth option is hypnotherapy, though it hasn't received as much attention as other methods. Hypnotherapy is when the person in labor performs hypnosis on themselves in order to achieve a meditative state in which to give birth under. It's meant to help ease pain during labor. This method requires constant practice and dedication, but it may be appealing to Pisces who want a natural birth. Others will find the idea terrifying and are perfectly fine with normal pain relief medicines available for birthing parents, and that's totally cool, too! What's best is whatever makes Pisces feel most comfortable and safe for themselves and their baby. The important thing is that their wants and needs are heard, understood, and abided by.

As parents, one of the most important lessons they'll have to teach their children is how to create and express boundaries. Everyone has to learn how to hold a proper container for themselves and others. This goes for the parents, too. They can easily slip into the mindset of being everything for their children, often losing themselves in the process. This cycle of dissolving the ego to serve others comes up many times in the Pisces lifetime. Adulthood and parenthood are no exceptions.

A Pisces unaware of the emotional impact they have on their children may end up projecting their suffering, dreams, and idolizations onto them. It is important to be aware of this risk because even the most well-meaning Pisces can fall victim to this mentality. Remember that children are their own separate and autonomous beings. They're not here to be what their parents couldn't. In fact, Piscean parents should know that no matter how old they are, they always have the magic power of mutability. They can be whomever they want to be! There's no need to project their desires onto their children, spouses, or anyone else.

PISCES

in Love

Piscean lovers tend to be idealistic, romantic, and very much invested in the idea of love. Pisces wants to be seen completely and fully by their beloved. They search for a love that defies the boundaries of space and time. They want themselves to be seen and accepted by their lover on a soul level. This aspect of life might prove to be one of the most difficult for Pisces, as their relationships are everything to them. They dream of the perfect partner and marriage from a very young age—someone who understands them from the inside out and who is just as devoted to love as they are. In short, they want a romantic type with whom they can create a beautiful life.

Unfortunately, it usually takes a series of disappointing love affairs before Pisces realizes what they really want and need in relationships. Pisces fall in love hard and fast; when they find someone who seems to meet their standards (which can seem low to others), they often fall into a dream state, putting their beloved on a pedestal while falling into patterns of devotion and idolization. Because of their fast descent into love-land, they can be seen as gullible and easy to deceive. This is especially difficult for younger Pisces, as they can easily fall into toxic or abusive relationships with people they feel they have a deep connection with. They enter relationships wearing thick rose-colored glasses, happy to have found someone who seemingly fulfills their fantasies.

Pisces must learn that a soul or fated connection doesn't necessarily mean everlasting love! They often attract other hopeless romantics and people with visible mortal wounds, as they tend to believe that they can fix anyone with love and affection! There's real danger in attracting people in need of fixing or healing. Pisces are so sensitive and absorbent they can easily become confused, not knowing if the feelings and emotions they are experiencing at any given time are theirs or their partner's. This can be truly detrimental to Pisces, who need to learn how to maintain clear boundaries between themselves and others to avoid both physical and mental sickness. They are subject to taking on the experiences of others because of their emotional vulnerability, their extreme sensitivity, and their transparency. There is no telling where Pisces ends and their partner begins. When their partner is sick or in pain, Pisces will subliminally take that on themselves as they try their best to heal the other person, often neglecting to take precautionary measures to protect themselves. The same goes for emotions. If their partner is angry or upset, Pisces may find themselves taking on those same feelings, most of the time without even noticing it's happening.

Because of their tendency to attract lovers who end up draining them of their magic and vitality, cycles of shame often manifest in their relationships. Their partner can make them feel ashamed for the loss of spark or fantasy that occurs when Pisces is worn down and drained of energy. This, in turn, can make Pisces even more cold and withdrawn, which means they'll be less willing to share themselves with their partner.

Pisces must learn that they can have soul-altering experiences with people who might not be "the one." Just because they have incredible sex or feel seen on an entirely different level doesn't necessarily mean that they're meant to stay with this person forever. It can be challenging for them to accept that they'll have many different types of lovers and varying types of experiences with love and relationships throughout their lives.

BEST SIGNS FOR PISCES

In terms of the type of person that's best suited for Pisces, they should look toward their opposite sign, Virgo, for some clues, as well as to their fellow Water signs, Cancer and Scorpio. Virgo is a mutable Earth sign, so, like Pisces, it is changeable and in concert with the flux of life. Because Virgo is an Earth sign, it can act as a container and help ground others in the reality of everyday life. Pisces need this balance in relationships—someone who can hold space for them, act as a counter to their ever-flowing, sensitive nature, and help keep them grounded on the material plane. Virgo also rules the process of critique and refined selection, something that Pisces often lacks when in search of a mate, since Pisces are very open and welcoming to almost anyone they feel a soul connection with. This isn't to say that every Pisces should be with a Virgo, but they should look for similar traits to help balance out their watery natures.

The other two Earth signs, Taurus and Capricorn, can be great matches for Pisces. They too can provide an earthy, stable, and comforting container for their water. Pisces, in turn, acts to nourish the Earth, adding magic, mysteriousness, and creativity to otherwise dry or stagnant earth. Together, water and earth make fertile ground, where creation and growth can occur. Being with an Earth sign allows Pisces to feel held and contained, which is comforting for a sign with emotions that change depending on who they're with or where they happen to be. The downside of Pisces dating an Earth sign is the potential for stagnation, as well as a lack of depth. Earth can be stable and secure, but will the relationship bore Pisces? For Pisces, the possibility of stability leading to limitations, boredom, or restriction is a constant fear. This can make them swim away quickly from relationships, often without much of a warning.

The strong, reliable container of Taurus can soothe Pisces' anxieties and fears of being left behind, but their slow-moving nature and inability to change might drive

Pisces crazy after a while. Tauruses move at their own pace, which is often quite slow and steady. They don't like to be pushed or prodded (think of a bull), and they will stay in one home, job, or relationship for decades out of comfort and fear of change. They're known for being stubborn, which Pisces quickly rejects. Their mutable nature can't fathom why someone would want to stay put for so long, especially when they aren't happy with where they are! Taurus's unwillingness to change, even when presented with ultimatums, can eventually be a deal-breaker for Pisces. However, if these two can find the right balance, a long-term union is easily possible. They'll enjoy spending time in nature together more than anything, perhaps growing their own food, cooking delicious meals, and building a fruitful life together.

Capricorns are alluring for their go-getter attitude toward life and career, which is particularly sexy to Pisces. Capricorn has the energy of a caretaker—someone who can provide material comfort and security for their partner. Capricorn and Pisces can create a meaningful life together, with Capricorn providing the material needs and

Pisces bringing the warmth, creativity, and caretaking to the home and family. However, will Capricorn's focus on career and financial stability prove to be too cold and hollow for Pisces? Pisces need to be able to share themselves fully with their partners, so plenty of quality time is necessary. Capricorn might not always be able to provide that for Pisces as they focus on building and maintaining their career status. Plus, Capricorns aren't exactly known for warmth and softness—quite the opposite actually! It isn't that Capricorns aren't emotional people. They just don't express it as much! Instead, it's usually kept inside, as their purpose is to build reliable structures to support their families and communities. This pair can last if Capricorn devotes enough time and energy to Pisces and makes them feel deeply noticed and understood. Pisces must also take care that they're aloofness doesn't throw off the otherwise grounded Capricorn.

With Virgo, opposites can definitely attract! The mutable natures of these two signs work well with each other because they're able to bend and change to adapt to new circumstances. Pisces' natural inclination toward dreaming and fantasy definitely contrasts with Virgo's connection to the everyday hustle and bustle of life. Virgo stays tethered to the earthly plane through their work, which is seen as service in their eyes. The daily give-and-take with the world around them keeps them grounded and sane. Pisces, on the other hand, also lead lives of service, but these are centered in connection, healing, and empathy. In fact, both signs hold natural healing abilities. Virgo is best equipped to work with the physical body, offering healing herbs and movement therapies for folks. They are gifted in paying attention to minute details and understanding the complexities of the human body in ways few others can. They are in tune with the body, whereas Pisces often strives to find release from the burdens of the body. Pisces are gifted in the art of healing what is unseen. This includes energy work, psychic abilities, empathy, and heart-centered connection. Both can heal, and together they can be an unstoppable duo! However, opposite signs are opposite for a reason! Although they can be categorized as two sides of the same coin, there is a tension between the two. Pisces can be exhausted by Virgo's relentless scrutiny and criticism. Virgo can easily become aggravated by Pisces' lack of boundaries and direction; they tend to drift through life, going wherever the wind takes them. This tension can lead to struggles and arguments in which the two find it impossible to see eye to eye.

It is, however, truly magical when two Water signs fall in love. Pisces can find a sense of connectedness with Cancer, Scorpio, or another Pisces that is hard to find with any other sign. In this combination, the two allow each other to feel noticed, held, and accepted on a deep soul level. Water signs just *get* each other, as they all hold the depth, psychic ability, and sensitivity of the element. They are able to nourish each other and understand the same fears, anxieties, and weird, mysterious abilities. They are all deep healers by nature and can offer this to each other. However, there is a danger of falling into toxic cycles, which is true in all relationships. Water signs share depth, which means that they can easily get lost in each other's issues. When Water meets Water, it is difficult to tell where one ends and the other begins. Serious boundaries have to be established early on, and both parties must make their intentions clear to the other so that a healthy relationship can develop.

When Pisces pairs with Cancer, sparks immediately fly. Both signs have a deep love for love itself, and they will probably find that their romance easily blossoms. Cancer makes Pisces feel held, soft, and surrounded by warmth and compassion. Pisces feeds off of Cancer's nurturing energy, which quenches Pisces' thirst for true love and connection. When Pisces feel the safety and comfort Cancers provide, they easily open up romantically and sexually. They feed off of each other's open-hearted energy. These two can have a world of fun together, often preferring to stay inside to cook delicious meals, have sex, eat again, and binge-watch their favorite movies together. Conflict begins when Pisces' capricious nature becomes too much for Cancer to contain. Cancers rely on emotional security. If Pisces appears too difficult to pin down or too much in flux, Cancer may give up on trying to secure a long-term relationship. Pisces, on the other hand, may find Cancer to be a little too nurturing and sensitive—yes, even for Pisces! Cancer is connected to the mother archetype, which may turn Pisces off if it becomes too overbearing.

Pisces and Scorpio is a truly mystical pairing—one that neither of them will ever forget. Pisces and Scorpios tend to have instant and penetrating connections. Often, they are immediately attracted to each other's deepest (some might say *baddest*) desires. Pisces mystifies and allures Scorpio with their big eyes and open aura, while Scorpio's mysterious vibe easily captures Pisces' attention. When they pair up, it's usually intense, as both signs have a deep urge to be understood on a soul level, and both are usually happy to form an intense bond when they find someone else willing to be with them. As with other Water signs, this pair can quickly become lost in each other's psyches and emotions, often seeming to communicate telepathically or through subtle gazes. Their sexual chemistry tends to be a major driving factor in the union, and they can both become insatiable for each other's deep love. This pair finds trouble when Scorpio becomes too intense for Pisces' mutable nature or when Scorpio, who can be a somewhat jealous and controlling sign, can't fully trust Pisces' staying power. If Scorpio can trust Pisces, and if Pisces can understand Scorpio's heavy and intense moods, they can find lasting happiness together.

When a Pisces meets another Pisces, the two fish are able to create magic that is truly out of this world! They are able to see each other as mirror images, seamlessly merging into each other's lives, like the blending of two oceans. Pisces may be taken aback by the effortlessness of the connection between the two, as they'll probably be able to understand each other instantly. Their fears, joys, and even senses of humor easily coalesce, and they quickly realize they've found something special in each other. The beauty and danger of this paring is the possibility of becoming lost in a shared fantasy. When this happens, neither one wants to come down from the high of deep, passionate, and endless love. Their connection can last if both parties have stable foundations to continue to grow from, and of course if they can maintain a level of separation between each other. It's all too easy for them to become lost in one another. The only way this couple can last long-term is if they both maintain a degree of independence. Certain parts of their lives must remain disentangled. The love and compassion these two signs can hold for each other is next-level, and it can be fostered through their shared ideals.

Pisces finds Fire signs to be exciting and alluring. Who doesn't want to stand next to a warm fire? Although Fire and Water don't typically mix well, there are always exceptions to the rule. Chances are good that Pisces will date at least one Fire sign in their lifetime. Water and fire can be hot and exciting, like boiling water! However, water and fire tend to lead to hot steam, meaning arguments will erupt and fizzle into nothing. This isn't to say that Pisces can't find love with a Fire sign! Pisces has a special connection with Aries; Pisces represents the end of a cycle, the last sign of the zodiac, and Aries represents the beginning, being the first sign. These two signs hold the energies of death and birth, last and first—the major threshold of endings and beginnings. Pisces finds Aries exciting and thrilling, like a shiny new car! Aries' energy and enthusiasm light something up inside Pisces that wants them to take risks, be bold, and follow their Aries into the sun.

Aries quickly relates to Pisces' mystical and mysterious energy, as Pisces makes them feel seen and understood. And indeed, Pisces does hold deep knowledge about Aries. The symbol of an ending must understand the magic of its beginning. Things may begin to fall apart when Aries becomes enamored with something (or someone) new. These Fire signs tend to have short attention spans when it comes to love, especially in their younger years. Pisces may eventually tire of having to tiptoe around Aries' ego. However, because these signs are right next to each other on the zodiac wheel, it's possible for them to share planets in each other's signs. For example, Pisces might have Venus in Aries, and Aries might have Mercury and Venus in Pisces; they share more of each other's traits than previously thought when one considers the Sun signs. A further analysis of both birth charts is always needed to determine true compatibility. If compatibility is possible, they should be able to build a lasting relationship together and have a ton of fun while they're at it.

Pisces and Leo have a unique connection with each other in that they share a love for fantasy, love, and beauty.

Like Pisces, Leos love to love, and they also lead life from the heart space. Both signs are highly creative and can bond over their obsessions with certain movies, artists, style trends, or celebrities. Pisces is enamored with Leo's playfulness, and Leo can't get enough of Pisces' eclectic, mystical energy. Their similar love for aesthetics and cuddling can take them far; however, a more substantive love will have to be the foundation of their relationship, or else it will become old pretty quickly. Although Pisces is able to give Leo the consistent love and validation they crave, Pisces can easily dull Leo's flame if they become far too depressing or sad for Leo's solar fire. Similarly, Pisces may grow tired of Leo's constant focus on themselves and how others perceive them. Pisces' caring and empathetic nature doesn't take well to people who are self-absorbed, and Leo simply can't stand anyone who may be blocking their light in any way. If their connection is rooted in something deeper and more substantial than aesthetics or sex, they can certainly have a long-lasting, happy relationship.

Pisces and Sagittarius have the ruling planet of Jupiter in common, which is present in both of their expansive

PISCES

and belief-oriented natures. They both have strong morals and ethics that they live by. Pisces may be more humanitarian, whereas Sagittarius is often more philosophical. These two can talk for hours at a time, ruminating on the meaning of life, social and political issues, history, or just about anything! They both have boundless natures that are difficult to contain. Pisces wholeheartedly looks up to Sagittarius for their incredible mind. To Pisces, Sagittarius can seem like the smartest person they've ever met! Sagittarius enjoys Pisces' sensitivity and openness. Sagittarius knows that Pisces won't hold them back from their adventures but will rather nurture, support, and accompany them wherever they go. Where these two falter is when Sagittarius fears commitment or can't see themselves with a long-term partner that is so sensitive to their brash quips. Pisces may eventually find Sagittarius too pompous or dogmatic for their taste. However, if both signs maintain a sense of security and stability with one another and understand that they don't want to hold each other back, then they can often find a lasting harmony that includes tons of laughs and fun experiences.

Pisces finds most Air signs especially exhilarating, intellectual, and hilarious. However, Air tends to lack depth, which is one of Pisces' biggest cravings. The air element rules communication of all forms, including speech, writing, and even thinking. Air signs inherently need verbal back-and-forth in order to process the thoughts that travel continuously through their minds. Pisces communicate through symbols, signals, art, music, and body language, while Air signs communicate through spoken and written language, equations and arithmetic, and facts and figures. However, this is by no means saying that Pisces can't end up with an Air sign. They have a lot in common with each of them. Pisces finds Gemini quite clever, funny, sociable, and entertaining. Gemini is a curious sign constantly mentally processing everything around them. Gemini's main concerns while going about their life are to gather information and make connections between these bits of information. Pisces is also constantly communicating, but usually subconsciously! While Gemini speaks as they think, Pisces generally doesn't have much to say, as they're always processing how they feel! These two can end up having a lot of fun together, staying up and chatting through the night or lightly debating topics of all types. Pisces enjoy the mental stimulation to a point, but this bubbly energy can quickly wear them out! Pisces really need to connect on a deep level, and this can be difficult with Geminis, who tend to hover around the surface. In addition, Gemini gets bored easily, and Pisces can't really be bothered to try and keep up. These two can last if they share common interests or if Gemini can get used to Pisces' sensitivities. Pisces must also get used to Gemini's restlessness!

Pisces has an affinity for Libra, a sign associated with partnership and union. Pisces finds Libra's beauty and sense of style especially attractive, and Libra is equally allured by Pisces' mysterious sensuality. Libra is ruled by Venus, a planet that thoroughly enjoys Pisces, and these two definitely share a keen interest in love, aesthetics, and fantasy. They both appreciate each other's impeccable taste and propensity to beautify everything they come into contact with. Libra's willingness to partner pairs well with Pisces' open heart, which is ready to give and receive love. Conflicts arise when Pisces feels that some of Libra's behaviors cause them to feel personal shame. Libra's often wishy-washy nature doesn't always mix well with Pisces' strong morals. Libra tries to argue both sides of a conflict, which can confuse Pisces and send them into a tailspin. Libra can also quickly tire of Pisces' constant confusion over problems and solutions that seem simple to them. However, there's a lot of potential here for long-lasting love if Libra possesses meaningful depth and if Pisces expresses their wants and needs clearly.

Aquarius comes right before Pisces, so they are next-door neighbors on the zodiac belt. They have a lot in common, notably their propensity to experience life from the margins of society. Both signs tend to have underlying feelings of being alone or of not fitting in with society at large, which includes their families and peers. They both long for human connection and acceptance of their true selves. Pisces and Aquarius have the potential to provide that for one another. Pisces finds Aquarius' oddities quirky and attractive, and Aquarius easily falls for Pisces' open and accepting nature. Aquarius can teach Pisces how to emotionally detach from situations in order to gain a broader perspective. Pisces can teach Aquarius the power of embracing feelings and diving into the full experience of emotions. Such developments are of course extremely difficult for these signs to imagine! Still, they can learn a lot from each other by exploring their differences. This partnership can start to go downhill if Pisces tires of Aquarius' rebellious nature. Pisces may find themselves thinking: "Aquarius seems to have an opinion about everything, and it's usually filled with disdain!" Aquarius may eventually become fed up with Pisces' constant fear and anxiety, in which case they'll have thoughts such as: "Just grow up already!" These two can make it work if Pisces maintains a degree of detachment and logic and if Aquarius learns to lead with love instead of criticism.

Whatever Sun sign Pisces ultimately ends up with, it's important that they see themselves as separate from their relationships and partners. This is the only way for them to have a truly satisfying union. Compromise is a given, but as long as Pisces is willing to stick with it for the long-term, beautiful relationships can be formed with any partner.

Hopefully the firm embrace of Saturn's Return teaches them the importance of boundaries, that boundaries are in fact love, and that structure does not have to mean limitations. Pisces must remember to only take on what is theirs, meaning that their partner's issues aren't theirs to deal with, worry about, or hurt from. They can empathize without embodying!

PISCES

at Work

Pisces are a true powerhouse when it comes to work and careers. Their inner fire begins to roar when they see the fruits of their labors. Pisces are hard workers unafraid to put in longer hours, and the results are usually bountiful! However, their true potentials are only realized when they're working toward something they actually care about. A Pisces will have many different passions over the course of their lifetime and will try many different jobs as they search for their purpose. Ultimately, Pisces yearns to alleviate the suffering of others, so they often seek out careers that allow them to feel as though they are achieving that purpose. Working with children, the elderly, the sick, the impoverished, or the disabled, and counseling are great places to start. They are not always the best at organizing or managing others, as their empathy can prevent them from becoming impartial and objective managers. However, they do excellent work behind the scenes, organizing stockrooms or tending to customer needs. Because of their mutable natures, Pisces often hold many different jobs at once, likely one that pays the bills and another that fulfills a certain passion or purpose. They can be quite adept at juggling multiple responsibilities as long as they remain organized and don't become too overwhelmed.

Pisces do really well when they are self-employed, as they like making their own money and being responsible for their own work. They are very self-sufficient in that way. However, this is only if they are able to develop a steady and reliable routine. Pisces, a mutable Water sign, isn't well-known for its self-starter energy. They can definitely be that way when they have an initial passion for a particular idea, but this can easily wane once they realize the hard work required to achieve their goals. It's not that Pisces is averse to hard work, it's that they often have a difficult time sticking it out for the long haul. New, exciting goals or distractions can pull them away from their original objectives. Because of this, having multiple jobs suits them well. They get the steady structure of a regularly paying job and the opportunity to explore other interests. For Pisces to be happy, this regular job should align with Piscean principles. Firstly, the people they work with must be openhearted and kind. Pisces should do their best not to subject themselves to toxic work environments, especially if they have to work in these environments most days of the week. They are simply too sensitive to be immersed in environments that are too harsh or whose employees lack empathy for others. Usually, if the people they work with are "chill" and get along with them, Pisces will stay with the job for a while. However, they do get bored easily! The Piscean mind must be constantly stimulated, otherwise it will resort to lofty daydreaming and escapism to help the hours pass. This can lead to depression and feelings of worthlessness, and Pisces would much rather keep busy with tasks that are helpful and necessary to the business rather than wander without direction or focus. Pisces need structure, consistency, and a healthy work-life balance in order to thrive in any position. Because of their extreme willingness to help others, they can easily fall victim to work situations in which the work becomes endless and their selflessness is taken advantage of. Pisces can easily feel as though they're becoming slaves to their jobs, especially when they lack proper boundaries at work. This is why being upfront with themselves (first and foremost) about what they will and will not tolerate in the workspace is important before beginning any job search. Of course, these critical-thinking skills probably won't appear until later in life, after some trial and error at different places of employment.

Pisces must be able to acknowledge the work they do and their value to their team or company in order to properly advocate for themselves. This includes asking for promotions and raises. These forms of direct confrontation with authority figures might be terrifying to Pisces, but they are necessary to prevent getting stuck in assistant or associate positions. Pisces needs to learn that they too deserve to be acknowledged for their work and fairly compensated. They may fear being seen as "rocking the boat" or disturbing the order of things, but it's crucial that they realize they're only doing a disservice to themselves by remaining in positions that don't allow them to grow. As stated earlier, it's important that Pisces is recognized for their work, otherwise they can grow bitter and resentful, which can lead to a lack of passion and desire to do good work. This can become a vicious cycle—Pisces starts to do less work to compensate for a lack of acknowledgement from their higher-ups. In turn their falling productivity keeps them from receiving praise or promotions.

Their main drive is to help others in some way. An adult Pisces has seen the world in all its beauty and horror. They've learned first-hand the power of love and compassion, and this is what they crave most. Above all, they have a deep understanding of equality. They believe we are all connected at the heart level and that human beings want love more than anything else. Pisces will feel unfulfilled in life if they are not working toward a cause larger than themselves. So, a mundane day job will likely have to involve helping people because Pisces has a hard time working for something they aren't passionate about. The pathway toward Pisces' ideal career can often be quite long and aimless, though some learn early on what they're meant to do. This really depends on the individual. Pisces are very powerful manifestors, so when they make their minds up about what they want to pursue, they usually have no trouble finding opportunities. Pisces' ability to

PISCES

manifest is often taken for granted or left unrealized. Once they recognize their power to almost seamlessly create the life they desire, they can start taking advantage of it. The main issue is settling on a path! Pisces are so mutable that their minds change easily, which can make them feel incapable of following through with their decisions. This can stem from a fear of failure or a lack of self-confidence in their ability to see their plans through. They know themselves better than anyone else, meaning they understand their propensity toward change. They often quit when challenges seem too difficult or "impossible" to solve. The thing is, Pisces should understand that choosing a direction is essential to their growth. This decision doesn't have to mean they'll be restrained in any way! The ability to manifest means that Pisces can create the life they want—the life that makes the most sense for them! In order to do that, it's important that they get specific. They have to take the time to acknowledge their present circumstances. They won't be able to manifest anything if they are in denial about their current state of being. For example, let's say Pisces is at a career crossroads. They're stuck in an office job they hate, but they have an idea for a coaching business. The first step toward manifesting their dream is to recognize where they're standing. They'll need to continue working another job in order to make ends meet while they build their coaching business. So, if they want to quit their current job, they'll need to manifest one that's in proper alignment to serve as a bridge for the next step. A Pisces acting too hastily might believe that manifestation involves simply asking for enough clients to go full time and then quitting the job they hate. A Pisces in tune with the power of manifestation would first ask for a job that fits their current needs in order to get them to where they ultimately want to go. For instance, they might have worked service jobs when they were a bit younger. Such jobs can provide the fulfillment and money needed to help bridge them to the next opportunity. As an adult, they have a clearer idea of the type of restaurant environment that suits their needs, so they can be even more specific in what they're asking the universe for. To get even more detailed, they can ask for the specific amount of money they'll need and the number of clients they can realistically expect to pick up as they're starting out. Specificity is the key to manifestation. Once the universe knows exactly what's desired, it can act accordingly to make it happen. Compare this to someone who simply "wishes" things would go their way. They say things like "I hate this job. I wish I could just quit and do my own thing." Wishing will only get Pisces so far, but taking meaningful steps toward manifestation actually works! After the specifics are figured out and a plan is developed, the next step is to let the universe know. Writing plans down on paper allows desires to be grounded in the physical realm, and saying them out loud helps speak them into existence. You get bonus points if this is done on a new Moon, which is a great time to set intentions for new growth. After this, a mixture of belief and action makes manifestation happen. Search for the job you desire, tell people about your plans so that they can help you along the way, and design and build your own website. Next, begin offering free coaching sessions to build up your practice, gather testimonials, and start building a clientele! Before Pisces knows it, they've landed a great new job that allows them the time and freedom to start building the business they want. Asking is key here—if you don't ask, the universe can't deliver. Another big part of this is engaging the community and letting friends and new connections know about the dream. The beautiful thing about Pisces is that the people around them truly want to help them succeed! Letting their community know about their dreams allows the universe to connect them with people who can facilitate quicker growth. Because of their ability to manifest, Pisces will typically never go without enough money, as they can usually find ways to make ends meet. This isn't to say it won't be difficult at certain points in life, but Pisces is so mutable and adaptable that they can usually discover new and creative methods of earning the money they need.

PISCES

in School

Pisces love to learn and absorb information. Issues with school come from incompatible teaching styles, too much pressure placed on the child, or emotional issues that accompany maturation. As stated before, Pisces' main learning style goes back to their need for direct contact with the subjects they're learning about. Teachers that engage all five senses in their lesson plans, show genuine empathy, and enforce strict boundaries will easily be Pisces' favorites. When they have a favorite teacher, they'll do all they can to impress them, including studying hard to get good grades, answering questions in class, and working hard to understand the material. Pisces are people pleasers after all, and they want to keep their authority figures happy, too.

In grade school, Pisces will love school. They particularly enjoy art and music classes (if they like their teachers), and they will often take their sweet time with their projects, enjoying being carried away by the fantasy they create in their minds while at work. Pisces can be slow learners, but that doesn't say anything about their levels of intelligence.

They're slow because they need a mind-body integration in what they're learning. They also need creativity infused into their learning environments in order to fully absorb information. Pisces aren't linear learners! They learn best when fully immersed in the subject matter.

It's easy for a Pisces student to compare themselves with others, as comparison is their natural method of self-refinement. It's important that they don't lose their sense of accomplishment and specialness when comparing themselves with other children. They must be consistently reminded of how special and unique they are in order to keep from feeling like they're never good enough. This isn't to baby young Pisces, but rather to acknowledge that they routinely have to be called back to their own identity, as they often reflect and embody the identities of others.

Grade school is the first place in which Pisces starts to form relationships outside of the family. As discussed before, Pisces has the potential to be very well-liked in school. They are easily adaptable, are empathetic, have few problems with sharing, and most of all, want to be liked! Making friends and forming connections comes very easily to them. They learn the power of flattery early on and find joy in complementing their peers. They thrive on making others happy.

But they'll also find that not every child shares their love-first nature. These sensitive creatures are easily hurt and offended. When accused of doing something wrong, they usually have to be told exactly what they did to make the other child cry or upset. Because Pisces acts from the heart space, they won't easily understand their wrongdoings. If shamed for hurting another kid when their intentions were pure, they'll quickly learn to internalize all criticism, which can be detrimental in the long-term. Pisces has to maintain an idea of themselves as "good" in order to move through their everyday existence. It's true that most Piscean children are at the very least *trying* to be good. It's up to the adults in their lives to explain why some of their actions may be hurtful and to let them know that it doesn't necessarily reflect poorly on their characters.

Boundaries are an ever-important lesson for Pisces of all ages, but their importance should be stressed at a very young age. Grade school is when Pisces should begin to practice boundary setting, as this will allow them to become well-versed in it throughout their schooling years and into adulthood. This practice is relatively new, as the millennial generation has made the word "boundaries" an important part of the idea of self-care. Teaching a child boundaries (particularly a Pisces) is important for many reasons. For one, it teaches body autonomy. Pisces' flowing, empathetic, and reflective nature can easily attract unwanted attention or bullying, and this can leave Pisces without a clear, defined way to separate themselves from their perpetrators. As a result, they may check out of their minds and bodies as a coping mechanism. Boundaries teach the young Pisces that they have control of their body and personal space. It also teaches them what it means to have those very important parts of themselves violated in some way. It's easy to show a child what this means—if someone pushes or hits them, they'll know a boundary has been crossed and that they should tell a grown-up. If a kid won't give them space when they politely ask for it, they'll know a personal-space boundary has been crossed and that they can ask for assistance from an adult. It seems simple, but making sure a Piscean child knows that they have this option is crucial, as they usually try to do their best not to cause trouble. Boundaries are an important practice in relationships as well, as Pisces is very susceptible to merging or mirroring the personalities of those they're spending the most time with. Pisces is a very reflective, adaptable, and mutable sign. Like chameleons, they can mold themselves to be like others without even realizing it. This becomes more relevant as Pisces ages into the teenage and adult years, when their relationships start bringing out their sometimes overly compassionate and feeling nature. It's hard for them to separate, detach, and become objective when they care so much about healing the suffering of others. Every now and then, Pisces needs to be reminded of their unique identity, as this helps them remember the personal authority they have in any given situation or relationship. They have a propensity to idealize their friends, putting them on pedestals and believing that they are better than they are. Praise for their individual contributions to class projects or correct answers to questions helps bring them back to themselves and fosters self-esteem.

PISCES

Middle school and high school are always difficult times for young people. It's a time of rapid development—physically, emotionally, and mentally. Because of this quickened and sometimes brutal period of growth, extra intervals of rest are essential. As children grow into teenagers, rest becomes harder to find, as they'll continuously spend time browsing the Internet and procrastinating doing their school work. Hanging out with friends becomes the preferred method of escape, and they'll immerse themselves in their respective friend groups more and more. Things that can help Pisces maintain their core identity through these years include the cultivation of a unique hobby, excelling at a certain subject in school, or playing a sport. Such activities help tether them and their ego back to themselves, which then allows them to create a sense of identity and accomplishment. Pisces sometimes needs to feel like a somewhat big fish in a small pond! Recognition is wildly important when it comes to school and work, as it helps them understand that their efforts aren't meaningless. It's easy for Pisces to feel disempowered and disenchanted during this time in their lives. Depression and anxiety are common in most teenagers moving through this stage of development. The underlying desire for Pisces is to be of service to those around them, but during this time, it can be hard for them to cultivate the reach their heart desires. They may begin to think, "What's the point?" It may be helpful to enroll a teenage Pisces in talk therapy if they desire, but keeping them active is key. They have to feel like they belong to something larger than themselves—a band, a sports team, a youth volunteer group, etc. In fact, Pisces can benefit greatly from the act of regularly volunteering, as they'll be better able to live out their purpose of helping others.

When it comes time for them to apply to colleges, they may resist the all-consuming nature often associated with higher education. Not wanting to be locked down, it's possible they'll opt for an environment that allows them room to grow their specific talents and ideals. They have big, lofty goals for their future, and they'll want to be in an environment that nurtures their curiosity to grow. It's also important to them that this environment hold morals and convictions similar to their own. This can look different depending on the Pisces, but a place that provides them with adequate structure is critical to their growth. They'll of course want as much freedom as possible, but too much freedom could backfire on them, as they are still growing into adulthood. In college, they'll quickly look to solidify a group of friends, as this will provide them with a necessary structure to lean on. Although there's danger in merging too quickly or too deeply with friends, this is a lesson they must learn during their soul's journey. Relationships are inherently a big part of Pisces' life in an educational setting, and it's likely they'll experience profound life transformations while in college. These are important years for them, as they'll be exposed to people different from themselves, learn about new cultures, and experience new things. These years will form the basis of their understanding of how the world operates. Because college can bring about such emotional experiences, learning is done very emotionally. During this time, Pisces learns a lot about the hardships in life, intense love, devastating loss, rebirth, and renewal. Adequate support systems are needed for Pisces to be able to move through this time with their heads above water. Sometimes it can just be too intense! They should be encouraged to stick through it as long as they're not in any danger. These processes will teach them a lot about life. Their friendships become their lifeline through troubling times, and this is where boundaries are extra important. Because of Pisces' empathy and compassion, they can easily be taken advantage of by other boundless people who seek to be heard and understood. Pisces may allow themselves to be too open with their hearts, their wallets, their homes, etc. without ever vocalizing their needs or boundaries within the relationship. These are tough lessons to learn, especially if their friends can't help them or if they're part of the problem. However, such lessons must be learned so that strong boundaries can be developed. Pisces need encouragement when situations like this take place. They must be reminded that they are not in any way at fault for being taken advantage of. The only person at fault is the perpetrator! Pisces just needs to learn how to become more discerning when it comes to who they allow into their inner circle. Tightening the ropes around who is invited to be close to Pisces is a lifelong lesson, but they'll come face-to-face with it during their college years.

As far as majors go, they'll want to pick a subject that allows them to explore the depths and undercurrents of humanity. This can include a variety of subjects such as art, creative writing, gender or race studies, psychology, biology, sociology, or even political science. They have the potential to dive deep into their studies—not necessarily for good grades, but rather out of an underlying urge to understand the subject at hand, that is, if they really care about it. Because of this, Pisces should be encouraged to study what calls them rather than what's deemed "sensible" or "responsible" by others. They'll find their way toward their destined career at some point. Forcing them to study a subject they care little about will do more harm than good, as they'll simply check out. Again, a college environment situated near nature is ideal, as it allows for a healthy escape from class and social stress. Pisces need to be able to regularly place their bare feet into the earth. This is an effective, yet simple method of recharging.

Many Pisces will want to pursue some sort of secondary education beyond college, but that doesn't always look like graduate school. Many find their true calling years after college, or at least after their major has been chosen. Pisces can become interested in topics such as counselling, spiritual or occult studies, therapy of one kind or another, social work, nursing, doulaship, or the arts. They'll find it necessary to pursue further education in whatever subject interests them, and they'll need the structure that an educational institution or mentor can provide. Eventually, Pisces will become a master of their own. Their dedication to learning, healing, and helping others will guide them toward a supreme level of understanding in their chosen subject. In time, they'll also be able to pass their knowledge onto others through teaching and mentorship.

PISCES

in Daily Life

As one might expect, these fish swim through each day relatively differently. Their mood determines everything, and their sensitivity is reflected in their varying moods. Pisces easily picks up the energies of their surroundings. This includes the person they spend a lot of time with, the person they've been arguing with online, and even the television show they watch before bed! It's important that Pisces learn how to cleanse and protect their energy field, as they are subject to increased risk of illness (spiritual, emotional, or physical) due to their sensitivity. When a Pisces is carrying the weight of another, they are at their weakest and most confused, as their symptoms usually don't match their reality. Some Pisces are unconsciously aware of this and close themselves off from the outside world for fear of being hurt by others. The fear and anxiety that consumes them can be overwhelming. A lot of Pisces were badly hurt in some way as children or young adults, and they often blame themselves and their sensitive natures for their pain. As a result, they may even deem themselves stupid or gullible and vow never to allow themselves to be hurt in the same way again. Little do they know that they're hurting themselves by remaining closed off. A fish does better in the ocean than in does in a tank. While Pisces is closed off to the world, they have little to bounce off of aside from their own fears, anxieties, and delusions. This can be dangerous! Pisces need a counterbalance—a strong, supportive community and healthy interactions with others. Friendships and community are some of Pisces' saving graces, as they provide a sense of structure for the otherwise boundless Pisces.

Still, Pisces must learn to protect themselves from certain people, as their open and compassionate energy seems to draw in particular types like a magnet! One such type is the energy vampire—a person drawn to sensitive types who are willing to take them in, listen to their woes, and offer advice and support. These energy vampires are especially good at draining Pisces' energy. Pisces is left feeling empty, confused, and tired after their interactions. The other person might feel relieved and recharged, but

Pisces is left trying to figure out why they're so achy and exhausted all of a sudden! Sometimes Pisces is left this way after an interaction with a friend or loved one. This is simply because they haven't learned to keep their energy field separate from the energy fields of other people.

There are many ways to clear and protect one's energy, including meditation, crystals, spirit guides, mantras, and affirmations. Meditation is a simple, cost-free tool that can benefit everyone. There are plenty of helpful guided meditations on the Internet, but here's a simple and easy one:

Make sure you're comfortably seated with your feet or seat firmly placed; this facilitates a feeling of groundedness. It's a good idea to do this in a quiet setting, but you can do it anywhere—on public transportation, in the shower, at the park, etc. Next, close your eyes and take a few long, slow, deep breaths. When you feel your body start to relax and your heart rate begin to slow down, start envisioning a shower of white light raining down on you. As it's falling, it washes away any excess energy that isn't yours to carry around anymore.

PISCES

Really imagine it. Feel it running down your face, down your shoulders and back, down your chest and stomach, and down your legs. Eventually it soaks back into the Earth to be recycled and regenerated. You can also begin imagining a strong, nurturing force rising from the Earth. It travels up your legs and spine, slowly moving through each of your seven chakras and cleansing you from within. Again, really try to imagine this! You can picture your root chakra (located at the base of your spin) as a bright-red ball of light. As this force encounters it, it begins to shine brighter. Continue to your sacral chakra. Imagine it as an orange ball of light, then move up to your crown chakra. *(A quick Google search for "7 chakras" will produce a ton of images and articles about the chakras, and they're worth learning about!)* Perform either or both of these exercises until you feel energetically cleansed, which may feel like a new lightness or sense of balance within you. This is the cleansing and clearing part. Now for the protection!

Next, imagine a glowing 360º sphere surrounding you on all sides, like you're inside a magical bubble made of light. You can imagine it as a protecting white light or as any color light you like, such as rainbow, blue, violet—whatever makes you feel safe and comfortable. Now think to yourself, or say out loud, "I only allow love into this space." You're now protecting your energy field! Try this exercise when you're feeling particularly low on energy, especially after being around a lot of people, doing a lot of socializing, or talking to one person for a long time about their personal issues. This doesn't mean you shouldn't do these things, it just means you have to acknowledge that you might be carrying some of their anger, grief, or sadness with you after you say goodbye.

Certain crystals can also be used to cleanse and protect your energy field. Selenite is a wonderful example. It's a white crystal often shaped into wands. Selenite is said to help cleanse the energies of the crystals it is placed around. It's also an excellent tool for cleansing personal energy fields. For an energetic cleanse, hover a selenite wand, or any shape of the crystal, over all parts of the body, starting from the crown and working downwards. It's helpful to imagine white light emanating from it and assisting in the cleanse. A crystal often used for protection is black tourmaline. It's known to have an absorbing effect, acting to block and capture energy that isn't serving or that's ready to be recycled. Many people keep black tourmaline in the corners of their living spaces to help protect their homes. Red jasper is a great stone to help keep Pisces grounded and connected to their roots. Carrying it can alleviate feelings of anxiety or stress. Wear it as a bracelet or keep it in your pocket.

Pisces' potential to take on other people's energy and issues is another reason why sleep, rest, and time to recuperate are so essential. They are often thought of as sponges, absorbing a little bit of everything and everyone they come across. Clearing their energy field and allowing the nervous system to return to base levels is so important for the health and vitality of a Pisces. They hold so much space for others, but they must remember that they can't continue pouring from an empty cup! Adequate time to check out, go into dreamland, fall asleep, and eat heart-healthy meals should be heavily prioritized. Of course, this can always be taken to the extreme, as many Pisces develop harmful escapist tendencies and patterns. Activities such as consuming drugs or alcohol, going shopping, or binge-watching TV shows aren't inherently "bad" or harmful, but they must be done consciously and never to excess. Pisces often have trouble with this, as they tend to be boundless people with few self-limitations. It's always helpful for Pisces to ask themselves, "Is this activity harmful?"

Discomfort and unease within the body are common parts of Pisces' life. Their ever-flowing, often-nebulous body, mind, and spirit are constantly reacting to their environments and the people around them. Therefore, barring illness or disability, pains of some type are usually present, but their sources are typically difficult to pin down. Pisces' mental health often suffers in conjunction with their physical health, but they aren't always linked. Suffering is of course part of being human. Whether it's physical, mental, emotional, or spiritual, some type of suffering is always taking place in every human's life. For Pisces, they seem to always carry some sort of suffering, or at least they're hyper-aware of their suffering and the suffering of others. Is this because they're so in tune with outside pain (even if it's hidden)? Or is it because Pisces, the last sign, is so close to the concept of death, finality, and the last stages of life? Such feelings are a heavy burden to carry, but Pisces has a tremendous capacity to help others through their understanding of suffering.

When Pisces begin to welcome and embrace the energy of their opposite sign, Virgo, they finally start feeling more whole and more in tune with the natural flow of life. Routine and structure truly allow Pisces to thrive, as they create a container for the watery, mystical energy of Pisces. Without this container, Pisces remains directionless, free to flow wherever the winds take them. An intentional Pisces who is able to create the life they want is a truly successful Pisces. Pisces benefits from a regular routine that allows them to connect with their body. They also need to consume grounding and nourishing foods. Their vitality is directly connected to these areas of life, and they'll easily become bloated, cloudy, unmotivated, or depressed when their health and wellness routines begin to slip. It's important not to feel shame when this occurs! No one is perfect, and routines can be really difficult to keep up with! Regardless, these are guidelines, not rules.

In the home, Pisces does best when living with other watery beings, as they need to be around people who can relate to and understand their deeply feeling nature. They need enough space for all of their things. They usually carry a lot of sentimental items, as well as a lot of clothes, shoes, books, and often plants, crystals, or other knickknacks that help them feel grounded in a space. They want plenty of windows and ample room to breathe. Pisces wants to feel cozy, but not trapped. Fish kept in tanks that are too small for them end up going stir-crazy! Pisces prefers natural lighting and soft, warm lights; nothing too bright or intense. Colored LED lights are great additions to any Pisces' home, as they can change the mood of the room to match internal moods. Pisces is all about setting moods within their home, aiming to surround themselves with beautiful items, smells, visuals, and sounds. Their home needs to be their perfect escape from the outside world. They need a place where they can easily decompress, sleep, and create. Part of creating the perfect vibe in their home is the music they play. In fact, one of the safest and most effective escapes for Pisces is music. Along with art, movies, books, and other ways of getting lost in fantasy, music is accessible and freeing. Venus, the planet that rules over the arts, music, and things of high value, is found exalted in Pisces, meaning that Pisces is Venus' favorite sign to hang out in! It's therefore easy to see why Pisces enjoys Venus' gifts. Music in particular can take Pisces to another level of consciousness. It allows them to lift out of their current state and enter a new world. Music envelopes their senses, awakens their heart, and penetrates their soul. Having a nice pair of headphones or nice speakers in their home or car is extra important! Music can set Pisces' soul free in a lot of ways. It also serves as a means for Pisces to fully express their deepest, most confusing or troubling emotions. Depending on the song, it can lift them out of dark places or send them there. Pisces usually finds music at a young age and attaches particular memories to certain songs, bands, or albums. Pisces enjoys living in nostalgia, sometimes listening to the music of their teenage years just to take themselves back to certain feelings, which they'll vividly reexperience. Some may find this confusing or odd, thinking, "Why would someone want to relive that time in their life?" Pisces gains a lot from returning to certain memories. This process allows them to reflect on their feelings and determine the best ways of moving forward.

Another important addition to a Pisces home is an altar or a special space for their most precious items. Pisces likes to find aesthetically pleasing ways of displaying their items, neatly arranging them with care and precision. This space is important, as it acts as a grounding force in the home, almost like a fireplace. It's important to clean and rearrange the altar every now and then, as it should reflect the changes Pisces is constantly experiencing.

Altars are an easy and fun way to work on manifestation as well. You can make an altar for anything—to attract money or a partner, to honor passed loved ones, or to celebrate a planet, god, or deity. You can also use them to celebrate yourself! There are plenty of tutorials online for making general or specific altars, but all you truly need are a few items that you cherish or that hold special significance for you. Arrange them in a way that feels intuitive and beautiful. You can add tarot cards, crystals, candles, photographs, flowers, nice fabrics, or other trinkets to this space—whatever feels aligned for you!

Another important piece to Pisces' home is its proximity to water, as Pisces has a close relationship with this element. Ideally they would live close to some sort of body of water, whether it's an ocean, river, lake, stream, or pond. However, keep in mind that flowing water is best. Even having access to a pool can do wonders for Pisces, as being immersed in or close to water helps their energy recharge and assists with their sense of vitality. If none of this is available, taking frequent baths or long showers helps. Baths are especially healing for Pisces. Adding salts, fragrances, oils, flowers, or herbs is a great way to enhance the experience. A lot of regeneration and recharging can be done this way, so it's extra beneficial! Pisces just needs to be sure to adequately moisturize afterwards to keep from getting dried out! Additionally, being close to some sort of observable nature is just as important. Pisces loves to be close to parks, beaches, woods, mountains, or anywhere they can go to disconnect from the world around them and reconnect to nature. They have a special affinity to animals and the basic processes of nature, so witnessing it in real time by smelling flowers, touching tree leaves, or simply walking barefoot through the grass is deeply healing for Pisces.

Lastly, a daily practice of some kind is immensely helpful for Pisces' everyday routine. There are so many types of rituals and customs that Pisces can explore, but it doesn't have to be complicated! For instance, taking five to ten minutes to center oneself every morning can be a ritual in itself. Adding affirmations, morning stretches, and a few minutes of meditation can go a long way toward improving your life. These suggestions can be modified to fit your needs, so they're a great place to start!

PISCES

in the World

Pisces have big goals for themselves and the world. They truly feel that they were sent to the Earth to help others heal. They'll easily become well-known amongst their friends, families, and communities as people dedicated to helping others in some way. Pisces aren't fully selfless, but they do believe in morality, justice, and fairness, as shown by Venus' exaltation in the sign. Pisces often feels called to attend to the most vulnerable members of society, taking particular causes very seriously. It isn't uncommon to find Pisces becoming doctors, nurses, vets, people who help rescue and rehabilitate animals, or environmental advocates. They can often be found volunteering or creating lives out of charitable work. For most Pisces who end up in these fields, they say they feel like they have no choice but to fulfil lives of service, as if they were born to help people. And whether its people or animals, Pisces is usually on the front lines helping them. One of the soul urges for many Pisces is to dedicate their lives to helping others. Their profound, empathetic natures find some sort of peace in this type of work, especially when they know their efforts to assist others are not in vain. There is often a spiritual component to this as well, as though the obligation to help has come from somewhere outside the physical world. This is of course a common teaching within most organized religions (think back to the discussion of Jesus Christ in the book's introduction). Like Jesus, there are similar figures at the center of all major religions, like Muhummad, the Buddha, Krishna, and others. Because Pisces often find a need for belief, faith, and connection of some sort due to their Jupiterian rulership, they are often drawn toward religions or other spiritual belief systems. They can thrive in these communities, feeding off of a collective sense of connectedness, faith, and a built-in framework of being helpful and kind to others—values that are inherent in Pisces already.

Beyond a connection to faith-based organizations or a life of directly helping others, many Pisces find that their purpose lies in creation. Whether it's music, visual art, performance art, creative writing, poetry, acting, design, or some other creative act, you'll find Pisces excelling at it! Pisces tend to be highly talented in arts of all kinds, drawing on their ability to slip into other worlds. Pisces' imagination is boundless. For them, creating a fantasy world in any shape or form comes relatively easy. You'll find Pisces behind some of the best movies, plays, and TV shows ever created—their ability to invent worlds is incredible! They're also adept at enchanting others through these unique creations. Pisces' capacity to draw people in stems from both their inherent magic and the appeals they make to the human condition. The worlds they create completely mystify their audiences, casting a spell on them powerful enough to make them believe they're really being transported to new places.

One famous, mystical, and alluring Pisces is Rihanna, who enchants her audiences through sensual music centered on love, heartbreak, and finding one's way toward self-acceptance. Her success in music has also led to the creation of a groundbreaking beauty empire and fashion line. Watching her sing and dance is a spell in itself, and her music videos always embody elements of fantasy, romance, seduction, and thrill while keeping viewers enticed with gorgeous visuals. Another Pisces is Justin

Beiber, who became an international pop icon at a young age. Discovered on the Internet, his popularity quickly skyrocketed. Young people all over the world are drawn to the empathy and sincerity in his angelic voice. He has the unique Piscean ability to be what his fans want him to be, appealing to them in a chameleonlike way. It becomes easy for them to project their fantasies onto him. His charm and likeability still enchant many across the globe. Another revolutionary creator of new realities was Steve Jobs, a Pisces whose dreams completely changed the way we communicate! This is obviously no small feat, as Steve Jobs worked tirelessly, and sometimes mercilessly, to see his dream, a fantasy at one point, become a reality. This is the ultimate goal for many Pisces—to make their dreams a reality. The inventions of Steve Jobs and Apple cannot be overlooked, as they truly did change (and continue to change) life as we know it. Kurt Cobain is another example of an enchanting soul whose art was widely appreciated around the world. Kurt Cobain's life ended in tragedy, but a lot can be learned about Pisces through a look at his life. His battles with mental health and depression were apparent in his music, and fans deeply resonated with the vulnerability he displayed in his art. An incredibly watery figure, his presence allowed people all over the world to acknowledge the difficulties of being alive—the suffering inherent in existence. He still remains a notable figure for his ability to display his deepest pains and wounds as beautiful pieces of music that other people can relate to. Writer Jack Kerouac was also a Pisces. His poetry and prose drew readers into moments of his life, almost like movies. His words could transform mundane memories into exciting, soulful journeys.

While Pisces are often known for their abilities to merge myth and fantasy with reality, they have an underlying desire to be known as conveyers of knowledge and truth. Many Pisces go on to be excellent teachers, counselors, life coaches, and motivational speakers. They have the unique ability to convey their empathy and understanding of suffering in ways that other people deeply appreciate and value. Their genuine kindness is easily felt by those they come in contact with, whether it's in person, online, or through their appearances as public figures. Pisces in particular have an underlying interest in psychology and philosophy, reading up on these subjects in order to build a more recognizable framework for the spiritual knowledge they already possess. They'll find that friends, family, and strangers seek them out for guidance and wisdom, often attracted by their "old souls" or the feeling that they've lived many lives. They tend to take this responsibility very seriously, choosing their words carefully so as not to introduce more harm into the world. They often cannot bare to know they've hurt another person!

Pisces' urge to pair their understanding with the complexities of the human soul becomes necessary as they aim to build the structures of a better world. Often, Pisces' dreams are rooted in utopian ideals. Many continuously ask themselves, "How can I help the world?" Pisces has big ambitions to improve the communities around them, but they also possess the vigor and dedication required to see them through. This is usually seen later in life, when Pisces has the time and means to better focus on their goals. They tend to be very altruistic, and they often feel compelled to make regular donations to causes and organizations that align with their interests and ideals.

The communities that Pisces builds throughout life are essential to their dreams, but they also help Pisces build a sense of personal belonging, support, and stability. As mentioned earlier, Earth signs are great for balancing out Pisces' emotional and sensitive nature, as they can act as a container for Pisces' water. Pisces also enjoys saturating Earth signs with their compassionate and mystical nature. Aside from simply having earthy friends, Pisces needs structure within the groups they are a part of. This means they must seek out involvement in communities and organizations that provide consistency.

In terms of communities and friendships, monthly meetups with different groups suit Pisces well, as Pisces can rely on seeing certain people on a regular basis—a practice that really helps ground their otherwise drifty personality. They'll want to be sure that the folks they surround themselves with have similar values and morals as they do. They can tolerate people of all different types, but not if they're mean or insensitive. They'll also want a group of close friends that makes them feel like they belong—a tough feat! Their friends will ultimately be people who won't judge them or try to "fix" them when they're at their lowest. Pisces needs friends that allow them to move through the waves of happiness, sadness, and everything in between without imposing their own beliefs on how Pisces should operate. They'll usually be able to cement a small group of loving and supportive individuals by the end of their Saturn Return (around age thirty).

CONCLUSION

As you can see, Pisces is a highly complex sign! Their complexities can be found in their elusive, mystical natures, and their simplicities can be reduced to a few statements about the power of universal love and compassion. Although this book has offered some generalizations about the sign, the aim has also been to highlight some of the universal qualities of Pisces' energy. Everyone has preconceived notions about the traits of their particular Sun sign, but those always come with layers of biases and assumptions based on the life of the individual. There is, however, an underlying commonality to each sign, and mysterious Pisces is no exception to this rule.

Not every Pisces is shy, introverted, empathetic, or creative. Not all Pisces make music, hug trees, or become involved in toxic relationships. Not every Pisces wants to be an artist or a healer. However, every Pisces does carry a particular sort of sensitivity within them. Every Pisces does yearn for a deeper connection to something larger than themselves, whether it's everlasting love, a higher power, or a lost past. Every Pisces needs adequate rest and retreat from the world around them so that they don't become anxious and overwhelmed by life's struggles. It's safe to say that most Pisces have an affinity to water.

In order to dive into the deeper layers of the sign, one can look to the tarot and the particular cards associated with Pisces and its energy. Tarot's addition to any astrology reading or discussion is helpful because it provides additional context through visualization. The images on any tarot card evoke something in whoever is bearing witness, and that resonance is deeply meaningful. The card associated with Pisces is the Moon. This might throw some for a loop, as the moon is usually associated with the sign Cancer, but the tarot's associations with astrology don't always fit into a neat box! In most decks, but particularly in the Waite-Smith deck, the Moon card features a large, full moon presiding over a body of water, presumably an ocean. The moon's glow is reflected in the shimmering water beneath it. Emerging from the water, almost framing the moon above, are two stone pillars jutting out toward the sky. In the foreground of the image are two dogs seemingly howling at the full moon above. A crayfish can also be seen moving to the water's surface, apparently attracted to the moonlight. This card takes us to a rather scary place—a deep, dark oceanic void. The Moon card presents a scene that is dark and wet. One might have a sense of drowning in an ocean of chaos. In the middle of the ocean, there's nothing to hold on to. Instead of thrashing around or attempting to tread water, one can lean into surrender. This card invites us to dive deep into the void, to have the courage to confront our shadows, and to hang out there while we gather a sense of centeredness. The Moon card represents the experience of stepping, or sometimes falling, into a void where it can be difficult to know which way is up or down. This card allows us to explore the depths of our being. The deeper we go, the more we're able to relax into the unknown. The more time we spend in the space, the better we're able to cultivate trust in our inner knowing and find our center in the darkness. Often referred to as “the dark night of the soul,” the Moon card draws us deeply inward, into a space where boundaries don’t exist. While here, we must learn to trust ourselves and our intuitions and navigate through a space devoid of linear direction. This seems to be part of Pisces’ major life lesson—to lean into the void and release the fears of unknowing. Faith and intuition are what ultimately lead them back to their center.

Another card connected to Piscean energy is the Hanged Man, which is ruled by the planet Neptune. Pisces and Neptune share similar significations, and this card correlates well to the Piscean experience. The Hanged Man, sometimes referred to by the gender-neutral “The Hanged One,” depicts a person hanging upside down from a tree branch. They are tied to the branch by one ankle, while the other ankle is bent ninety degrees, similar to the tree pose in yoga. This person’s face appears calm and serene, and a glowing halo surrounds their head, symbolizing a state of enlightenment. This card illustrates the powerful act of total and complete surrender. We see the figure on the card in an extremely uncomfortable position, yet they’ve managed to move past their physical discomfort, surrender to their situation, and achieve enlightenment in the process. This card comes before the Death card in the tarot, marking it as a gateway to transformation. In the tarot, Death is rarely a symbol of physical death, but rather a symbolic ending leading to a profound transformation. The Hanged One prepares the soul for this transformation. The meditative state depicted in this card encourages acceptance of the letting go that's to come. Again, the relation to Piscean energy is stark, as Pisces often find themselves in this state of surrender as they move through life's major thresholds. Pisces are gifted with the ability to dive deep into their psyches, like in the Moon card, and surrender to the discomfort of not knowing what comes next, like in the Hanged One card.

Finally, a discussion of tarot cards related to Pisces wouldn't be complete without discussing the Queen of Cups. This card represents a person or a quality within a person deeply connected to their intuition. The Queens in the tarot are all sensual and nurturing beings who have done the work of discovering their inner magic, which they radiate outward to all who are fortunate enough to bear witness. The Queen of Cups represents a state of highly psychic, nonverbal communication and deep knowing. They are able to dive deep into their psyches, drawing on their keen intuition to receive information from other realms. They are deeply nurturing and mysterious, and can hold sacred space. This card represents a mature Pisces who has fully developed their deeply creative and intuitive gifts. When such a state is achieved, Pisces is able to help others from a place of knowing and centeredness.

Pisces everywhere should know and honor their abilities to create magic wherever they go, help others to see the magic in themselves, and show the world what true compassion and service look like. As long as they learn to take care of themselves first and foremost and navigate through this mysterious world with empathy and trust, they'll be able to make their dreams a reality.

INDEX

PISCES

ABOUT THE AUTHOR

Astrology has always held a place in Shakirah's heart. At a young age, her father, a fellow Scorpio, began quizzing her on the planets and their order from the sun. By the age of eight, she already had the names of the celestial bodies in her vocabulary. For as long as she can remember, she has found birthdays to be particularly special. She took great pride in knowing the birthdays of her friends, classmates, and family members. Even back then, she took note of the time of her birth, believing that this information would one day be important. In high school, she would buy birthday books to bring in and show her classmates, who nodded along as their minds were blown by the accuracy the books displayed. Whenever she's asked about learning astrology, she describes it as a remembering, as if this knowledge

PISCES

were information she had known previously, perhaps in other lifetimes. Sparks went off the first time she saw her birth chart in 2012, and she immediately knew she had found something special. She describes her first time seeing her birth chart as being "witnessed by the universe," a divine and cosmic experience. She was hooked instantly, and she didn't sleep that night, as she was too busy relearning this cosmic science. Astrology quickly became the lens through which she views the world, and she hasn't looked back since!

Through the years, she's poured herself into the subject, aiming to learn as much as she can in order to fulfil her passion of sharing this information with others. In her opinion, astrology is an invaluable tool available to people of all backgrounds. Shakirah currently lives in New York and takes clients online. She is the founder and editor in chief of *NFLUX Magazine*, an independent astrology and culture publication that features interviews, horoscopes, embodiment sections, and so much more. In addition, she hosts a monthly meetup for local astrology enthusiasts of all levels called Deep Seekers. She also organizes monthly dinners for New York-area astrologers to connect. She teaches workshops, hosts lunar circles, and writes horoscopes. This is her first book. You can find more information about Shakirah and her offerings at www.thestrology.com, or on social media: @thestrology.

OTHER BOOKS IN THIS SERIES

Zodiac Signs: CAPRICORN
DECEMBER 22–JANUARY 19

Zodiac Signs: AQUARIUS
JANUARY 20–FEBRUARY 18

Zodiac Signs: PISCES
FEBRUARY 19–MARCH 20

Zodiac Signs: ARIES
MARCH 21–APRIL 19

Zodiac Signs: TAURUS
APRIL 20–MAY 20

Zodiac Signs: GEMINI
MAY 21–JUNE 20

Zodiac Signs: CANCER
JUNE 21–JULY 22

Zodiac Signs: LEO
JULY 23–AUGUST 22

Zodiac Signs: VIRGO
AUGUST 23–SEPTEMBER 22

Zodiac Signs: LIBRA
SEPTEMBER 23–OCTOBER 22

Zodiac Signs: SCORPIO
OCTOBER 23–NOVEMBER 21

Zodiac Signs: SAGITTARIUS
NOVEMBER 22–DECEMBER 21

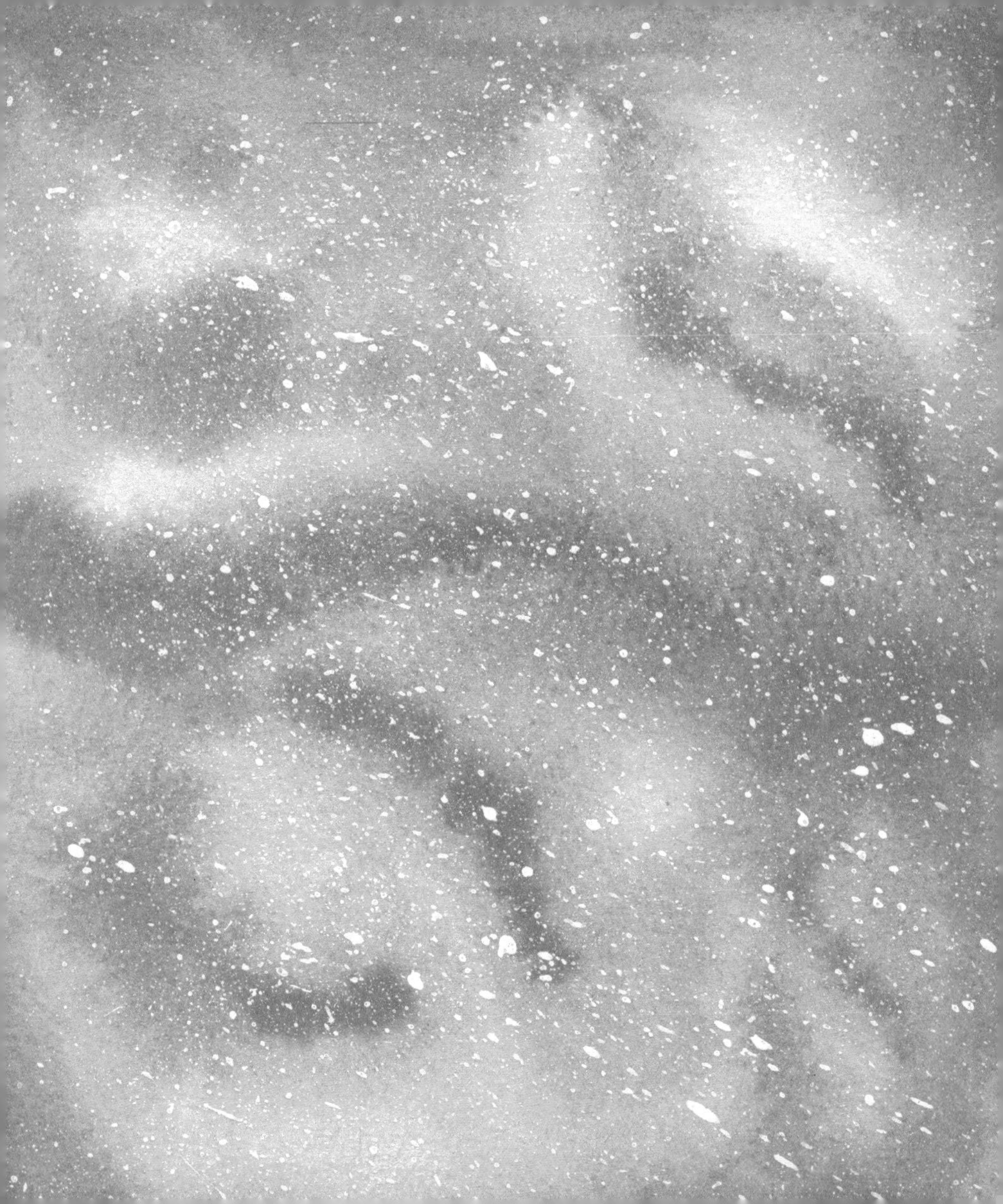